I0076889

Acknowledgements

I would like to thank Shuronda Robinson my Life Coach, Zanna James, Ken Barkin, and Susan Chiu for your support and encouragement while completing this book. Thank you Julia Chambers for the book cover design and Presenter Media for the art work.

ISBN - 13: 978-0692297551

ISBN – 10: 0692297553

All inquiries should be addressed to:
RealtorBiz101
C/O Trisha Miller
9604 Curlew Drive
Austin, TX 78748
(512) 773-5775
trisha@RealtorBiz101.com

See Page 87 For Your Free Service Offer

Disclaimer

This publication is to give the For Sale by Owner information on what to expect and what might be needed throughout the sale of their property. The information contained in this book is general and for informational purposes only and may not apply to every situation. Each real estate transaction is different due to the buyer and seller's needs and the contract specifications.

This publication is not intended to replace or discredit any Realtor or be a substitute for legal advice from an Attorney. It encourages the seller to speak with a Realtor, Mortgage Lender, or Real Estate Attorney with their questions depending on their situation. The author provides no warranty and does not guarantee the sale of your home.

See Page 87 For Your Free Service Offer

Table of Contents

See Page 87 For Your Free Service Offer

Introduction

How to Sell Your Own Home was written to help you, the for sale by owner, understand where to take precautions placing you in a better negotiating position concerning the sale of your home.

This book is intended to demystify questions that may arise in the selling process. It explains the importance of coordinating specific dates or the number of days to tighten up any loop holes that could give the buyer the opportunity to walk away from their initial offer.

This book covers:

- Getting Ready to Sell Your Home
- Negotiating An Offer
- Executed & Receipted Contracts
- The Option Period and Home Inspections
- The Appraisal and Survey
- The Mortgage Process
- The Title Commitment
- Marriages, Divorces, and Probates
- Tenants and Temporary Leases
- Property Taxes and Home Owners Associations
- Selling Modular and Manufactured Homes
- Financially Distressed, Short Sales & Foreclosures
- Closing Day and the HUD 1 Statement

See Page 87 For Your Free Service Offer

Not all of these subjects may apply to the sale of your home but most will. This book is intended to give the owner a fuller understanding of what needs to be done if you have never sold a home without the assistance of a Realtor. If questions arise concerning the real estate contract or transaction do not hesitate to seek the advice of a real estate professional in your area.

I hope you find this book informative and wish you the best of luck on selling your home yourself.

Preparing To Sell Your Home

There are numerous reasons a home owner would want to sell their own home and there is much to consider in this process like preparing your home, determining an asking price and what paperwork you might need. There is much to think about and take into consideration.

This chapter will cover, preparing your home for the sale, resources for helping to determine a sale price, documents you will need handy, advertising your home for sale, and other services some real estate companies may offer that could be to your advantage.

The Appearance

The presentation of your home is the first thing to catch a buyer's attention. How your home looks is important. If it does not look appealing on the outside a lot of buyers will pass it by and move on to the next one. Buyers tend to think; if the home doesn't look appealing on the outside it must be worse on the inside. This may not be the case but that is how most buyers think. If the buyer is looking for an investment, their thoughts might be along the lines of, this house appears to need work, I wonder how low of an offer they will accept?

Outside

Your curb appeal needs to be inviting. Adding life, color, and a sense of welcome to your yard will make it much more appealing. The fresher your home looks on the outside the more inviting it will be to a potential buyer.

Start by cutting the grass, trim the edges, hedges and trees; and remove dead plants from the yard. Power washing the outside of your home, driveway and sidewalk will clear off weather residue or any spots left from cars parked in the driveway.

Clean the gutters of any dead leaves if you have them and secure any loose areas. Repair or replace any damaged trim or edges around your home. Don't forget to clean the windows, sliding glass doors and repair damaged screens if you have them. If a fresh coat of paint is needed, do so.

Inside

On the inside there is much to consider in preparing your home for sale. Not only is it important how it appears but also how it smells. The condition of the appliances, hot water heater, air conditioner, and heater are equally important.

De-cluttering the home will make it look more spacious. If you have large antique furniture in a small space or wall to wall furniture because you

See Page 87 For Your Free Service Offer

have outgrown the home, consider putting some of it in storage. When de-cluttering your home, keep in mind you want the potential buyer looking at your home not your personal belongings. Buyers will look in your closets to see how much room there is for their clothes and personal belongings. The same is true for your cabinets.

You are planning a move and this is a good time to consider how much you want to take to your new home. The closest thrift store will be happy to receive items you have decided to let go of. Donations to charitable organizations are a good thing and some will pick up what you no longer want.

If you have a home office space pick the papers up off the floor and keep the desk area as clean as possible. If you do not have adequate storage in your office area consider purchasing decorative boxes from a craft store to put your papers in when you know a potential buyer will be viewing your home. Remember to turn your computer off before the viewing. Small children love to press buttons.

Smells

The fresher a home looks and smells the more appealing it is to a buyer. Weather permitting, open the windows and let some fresh air in or use an air

See Page 87 For Your Free Service Offer

freshening sheet on your air filter. You should be able to find them were you purchase your air filters. This is an inexpensive way to continually freshen the air in your home.

Keep the kitchen and bathrooms as clean and odor free as possible. Empty trash cans often and keep the dirty clothes in the hamper or laundry area. Be mindful of the dirty dishes stacking up in the sink.

If you have pets or smoke in the home be aware that some people have allergies to pet hair or dander and tobacco smoke. If your pet is shedding make sure to remove pet hair from carpets and furniture before a potential buyer views your home.

Personal Belongings

One thing to consider before showing your home to a potential buyer is the placement of your valuables, money, any forms of identity, and medications. If you work from home put away any confidential information you might be working on. Always keep in mind your allowing strangers into your home. You need to keep these things out of sight and reach. If you do not have a safe or file cabinet you can lock these items in, put them in a box and lock them in the trunk of your car.

Another thing to consider concerning your personal belongings are the photos you take of your

See Page 87 For Your Free Service Offer

home when advertising on the internet. Take care not to include photos with your electronic equipment, valuable musical instruments, hunting equipment, jewelry boxes and things of this nature. Keep in mind your selling the house, not your personal belongings. What you place on the internet can be seen by millions of people.

Repairs

You may be aware of repairs that need to be taken care of but if the property was previously a rental home or something you inherited, you may not be unaware of the home's working condition. If you're not sure, give a home inspection company a call. Having a home inspector come out, inspect your home, and give you a report will be well worth the peace of mind and expense.

Should you choose this option; the inspection report will let you know any issues that may need to be addressed. The more you take care of before a buyer makes an offer, the less they will ask for in repairs or try to negotiate a price reduction in lieu of repairs.

In most cases the buyer will have their own home inspection done on the property before they purchase the home. Once they receive the inspection report they may want to renegotiate the purchase offer concerning repairs or a price reduction. If you

See Page 87 For Your Free Service Offer

previously had the home inspected you will not be surprised by any repair request that you have not already addressed. If you provide a copy of your home inspection and invoices for repair work that has already been done, they may accept your inspection report and skip the option period in the contract.

Most inspectors charge by the square footage so be sure to ask about this when researching inspection companies. This one step could save you needless headaches, time and money.

Determining the Price

When you choose to sell your home yourself, you will need to do some research before you put a sign in the yard. You'll need to find out what the fair market value for your home is. Don't rely on the tax value to be the fair market value. Your home could be worth more or less depending on the rise or decline of values within your community.

Don't rely on conversations with your neighbors to determine the value either. What a neighbor asked for their home may not be what they were offered. You may have discussed with others in your neighborhood what their home sold for. If they gave you a casual answer like "We got what we wanted." or "We're happy with the price." does not mean that they got the price listed on their flyer.

See Page 87 For Your Free Service Offer

Two options to determine the fair market value of the property is to contact a few real estate agents and ask for a Market Analysis. Most of the time realtors will not charge for a Market Analysis. After speaking with a few Realtors you will have a good idea on the amount you should be asking for your home. Another option is to have a professional appraisal done.

You may already know a Realtor you can use for a market analyst and suggested sell price. If not, you could ask someone if they would refer you to a real estate agent.

When you call to schedule an appointment for a market analysis or appraisal, be prepared to answer a few questions. These questions will enable them to prepare more thoroughly for your time together. They may ask you questions like how many bedrooms, bath rooms, square footage, the lot size, or questions about additional amenities to the home. This is basic information they will need in order to prepare their values for your home.

Some real estate agents may prepare a net sheet for your review so you can see the estimated proceeds based off the suggested sale price. If you choose to answer any questions concerning your mortgage balance, it does not need to be an exact amount; it is only an estimate used to calculate your net proceeds. If you feel uncomfortable answering these questions, decline to answer. A net sheet is something that can be calculated once you are presented a purchase offer. This is also something a title company can prepare for you, when the time comes.

Other Services Some Realtors Offer

Some realtors offer a variety of services with different fees for each service. They may offer to place information about your home in the multiple listing systems (known as the MLS or MLX). They may have a variety of packages that would be more flexible with your needs should you choose to take this into consideration. They may also provide a variety of payment options for services rendered.

Real estate agents that work on commission or flat fee basis normally do not collect any payments for their services until your home is sold. Should the house not sell for any reason you owe them nothing that was not previously agreed to.

Disclosures and Warranties

Now that you have determined an asking price consider having paperwork handy concerning the condition of your home. These documents could include any warranties for past work done on the home or appliances you may have recently purchased. You might also have inspection reports or appraisals, a survey, or diagrams of the home or land. If you have any documents like this have copies handy, some buyers are very interested in this type of information concerning the home they are considering purchasing. Keep them together in one place so you can find them easily should you be asked.

If you were to use a Realtor to list your home for sale they would ask you to fill out a Seller's Disclosure. Though these forms may feel time consuming they were designed to help protect the seller and inform the buyer. Even though the buyer may ask to have the home inspected, a Seller's Disclosure is additional information should something come up later. Two places you can get these forms would be a Realtor, or you state's Real Estate Commission. There is also a lot of information available on the internet.

You want to position yourself as having disclosed as much information to the buyer as possible. By having something in writing, signed and dated by both the seller and buyer will help to protect you should something come up after the property has been sold. It would insure that you, in good faith, had informed the buyer of everything you knew about the home before it was sold. If the home was built before 1978 you will also need to include

See Page 87 For Your Free Service Offer

information concerning any possible Lead Based Paint.

Get your hands on a Seller's Disclosure, fill it out and make 3 or 4 copies to give to potential buyers. When a buyer makes an offer be sure to have them read, sign, and date the Seller's Disclosure; keep a signed copy for your records and give a signed copy to the buyer.

You may be able to get these forms from the Real Estate Commission within your State. Every state has a Real Estate Commission and some offer free forms to the public that can be down loaded from their website. Another option would be to search the internet, be sure to include your state so you get the correct forms for your area. If you can't find one contact a local Realtor or Mortgage Lender they will be happy to provide the forms for you.

Marketing Your Home

Putting a flyer box in the yard, letting your friends know and advertising it on all the social media sights you belong to is a good start. You will need to decide how else you intend to let people know your home is for sale. There are a number of "For Sale by Owner" websites you can advertise your home on, and many of them are free. Below are a few easily found on the internet:

See Page 87 For Your Free Service Offer

- Owners.com
- Fizber.com
- Forsalebyowner.com
- FSBO.com
- Buyowner.com
- Zillow.com/for-sale-by-owner
- Trulia.com
- Salebyowner.com
- Forsalebyownercenter.com

You will need to take some good photos to upload onto a website, write a description about your home, neighborhood amenities, and things you like about the area. Don't forget to include your contact information.

When taking photos make sure to remove any valuables, medications, or personal belongings you don't want advertised. Keep in mind that you are posting information to the internet and you need to be aware of what other people will see.

Qualified Buyers

Once a buyer is ready to make an offer on your home you will need to find out if they are qualified to purchase the home. If the offer is being presented by their Realtor most likely the Realtor has already been in contact with the buyer's lender or confirmed they have the finances available to pay cash for the

See Page 87 For Your Free Service Offer

home at the closing. Simply ask the Realtor for written verification the buyer has either been qualified by a lender or has the necessary funds with a financial institution.

If the buyer is presenting the offer themselves you will need to ask them for written proof they are eligible for funding or have the funds to provide cash the day the transaction is completed. This written document should be on company letterhead with the lender or person who can verify this buyer is eligible for a loan or proof of funds, and include their contact information. Check to see if the letter is dated. If there is no recent date on this document you may consider contacting the person who signed the letter to verify the buyer's status has not changed.

Another suggestion is to contact your lender, bank or credit union and make arrangements with a Loan Officer that they will speak with and prequalify any potential buyers should they not already have a lender. You want to position yourself where you are accepting an offer from a buyer that is ready, willing and able to purchase your home.

Now that you have prepared your home, gathered all the documents you need and have an interested buyer; the next step is negotiating their purchase offer.

See Page 87 For Your Free Service Offer

Negotiating An Offer

There are different types of buyers that may be looking at your home and considering purchasing the property. There are investors, realtors, and the consumer. One thing they all have in common is they are looking for a good deal. The majority of buyers prefer to use a licensed real estate agent to represent their best interest.

Investors and realtors are considered professionals in the field and have resources to determine the market value of the property. After they review the information, in most cases, they will offer you a lower amount. They will be considering how much profit they can make off a tenant or may be considering remodeling the home and flipping it for a profit.

Sometimes, when an individual consumer shows interest in your home, they have a realtor they're working with. Realtors may ask the buyer to sign a Representation Agreement – meaning the buyer has professional representation.

The Representation Agreement is an exclusive agreement between the agent and buyer, this allows the agent to research homes that are for sale, including For Sale by Owner's, and help the buyer through the purchase process of a home. They will act in the best interest of their client. This agent

See Page 87 For Your Free Service Offer

must disclose any information that they know about the property to their client, including information that you may give them.

In most states the seller is the one to pay the agents fees. Be prepared for the agent to ask you to pay them a commission or a flat fee. If you are willing to pay this agent it should be deducted from the profits of the sale at the time of closing, not in advance. In some states each person pays their own agent for services rendered. In this case the buyer will take care of the financial arrangements concerning compensation for their realtor's services.

If neither party is willing to pay the buyer's agent, be aware that the buyer may not feel comfortable purchasing a home without professional representation and continue searching for their dream home elsewhere.

Contract Loop Holes Overview

When selling your home yourself you can choose to have a lawyer create a contract for you, purchase some online or at the local office supply store. Some states offer free use of their standard real estate forms that have been approved by the governing Real Estate Commission in your state.

If you choose to create your own purchase contract it would be wise to pay a licensed real

See Page 87 For Your Free Service Offer

estate attorney to review the document to ensure nothing has been missed.

Should you choose to use the regulated state forms, there will be blanks to fill in and boxes to check. Since these blanks are negotiable they can create loop holes allowing the buyer multiple opportunities to back out of the contract. You need to be aware of these loop holes and how to tighten them up.

There should be a number of days or dates to fill in concerning:

- The Executed and Receipted Dates
- The Option Period
- Home Owners Association Documents
- The Survey
- The Lender's Final Approval
- The Closing Date

What dates or number of days and their placement on the purchase contract are important for you to be aware of. Please note that the above list may not include all the spaces that need to be filled in. This could vary depending on the Addendums and Amendments that are attached to the contract you are working with.

When there is too much time between days or dates it will give the buyer more opportunities to say I've changed my mind. Below are some day ranges that you may want to consider. Each one of these topics will be addressed in more detail throughout the book.

- The Executed Date – This is the day that all other dates and time frames within the contract revolve around. This is the start date not the Receipted Date. The Receipted Date is the day the Title Company receives the contract and earnest money check.

- The Option Period – 7 to 10 days are the average amounts of time asked for unless there are additional issues that need to be inspected that may take more time. Such as a professional septic inspector from the county or MUD District, a professional roofer or an engineer's report concerning the foundation. Keep in mind that holidays or bad weather can delay inspections.

- The Seller's Disclosure – you should already have one filled out. It would be to your advantage to provide the Seller's Disclosure to the buyer before their inspection. If you don't have one and they ask for one you should be allowed a certain number of days to get them the disclosures. If the buyers ask for a disclosure and you do not provide one for them, this is an opportunity for the buyer to say you didn't provide requested information and walk away from the agreement.

- The Survey – you only want to have a few days here. If a survey has to be ordered it will be the last thing done by the lender before you sign closing documents. Three days is normally a sufficient amount of time after the title company, lender and buyer have received the survey. Tis should be enough time for any objections to be mentioned. An exception to this might be through the holiday seasons.

- HOA Documents – the buyer should receive these within the same time frame as the number of days allowed for the home inspection. You will need to get these documents from your home owner's association. <u>You will need to ask for the Rules, Regulations and Bylaws along with a Resale Certificate.</u> Make sure to find out from your HOA how much the transfer fee is. Some are quite high and you may want to split that cost with the buyer. In some cases there may be an additional fee for a copy of the documents you are requesting, so you may want to have the HOA fee structure before you finalize a purchase offer.

- The Lender's Approval Date – This will be the date or number of days the lender will need to process the loan application, obtain all the necessary documents, submit them to the underwriter, and receive final approval. This process should take around 21 to 30 days depending on how much work has already been done before the lender receives the purchase contract.

    If the buyer is applying for an FHA or VA loan, be aware that sometimes these types of loans can take a little longer to process. The approval for FHA or VA loans could take up to 45 days.

No matter what contract you use get everything in writing, signed by all parties, and give a copy to the buyer. That way there are no questions on what has been agreed to and the buyer will have a copy for their lender.

Executed & Receipted Contracts

The executed date is the day that all parties agree to everything in the contract. This is the day that all other days and dates revolve around. In most states contracts <u>the number of days are weekdays not work days</u> – meaning 7 days a week - not Monday thru Friday. The days should start in effect the day after the executed date of the contract. Be sure to read the information about the executed date carefully.

Example: If the executed date is May 1st the counting of the days for time purpose starts on May 2nd. If in the option period you gave the buyer is 7 days, the last day of their option period would be May 8th.

Once you have a purchase contract that has been agreed to and signed, someone will need to take the contract and earnest money to the title company. It is in your best interest that the earnest money is held by a neutral party and not the buyer's agent or their real estate company. The earnest money check should be made out to the title company or the real estate attorney's office that will be closing the transaction for you. They will receipt the contract and take the check. The earnest money will be deposited into the company's bank account and held until the closing day. The HUD 1 Statement will reflect the earnest money deposit when closing documents are signed.

See Page 87 For Your Free Service Offer

Both you and the buyer will need a copy of the contract for your records and to stay on task with all the days and dates. It may be easier to remember everything if you mark these important days and dates on a calendar or in you planner.

The title company will perform a title search to make sure no one else has any claims on the property and to ensure that all current liens and property taxes are paid in full at the completion of the transaction. The closing company will pay these debts form the profits on the sale of your property. They will also be responsible for giving you the remainder of the proceeds – your profits.

Before you sign closing documents the closing officer will need to get the lenders name, loan number, and social security number of the person whose name is on the loan. They need this information to get payoff information and to verify the account.

There may be other documents the closer will ask for in the event any of the following subjects pertain to your situation. Below is a highlight of situations where more information will be needed by the closing company.

Similar Names

Should you have a common name like John Smith; there may be an issue with another John Smith that is not you and it may show several liens that need to be paid. <u>Do not worry!</u> This is easily corrected by your social security number, a different middle name, a different spelling and things of this nature. You may be asked to sign an affidavit stating that you are not that the other person. In most cases this situation is easily rectified.

Married or Divorced

If you have divorced since you purchased the home you will need to provide a divorce decree stating that you have the right to sell the home. The ex-spouse may need to sign documents depending on the laws in your state or what is stated in your divorce decree. If they are entitled to any money from the sale of the property it will be paid to them at closing.

If you have married since the property was purchased your spouse may also need to sign closing documents or an affidavit stating that they are aware you are selling the property and agree to the sell. You may also be asked to provide a marriage license. This is determined by your states laws.

Deaths, Wills, and Probate

In the event an owner has deceased and you are the executor of an estate, the title company will ask for:

- Probate documentation
- A copy of the death certificate
- A copy of the will
- Executor or Power of Attorney documents

If the property needs to be probated, it needs to be complete before the property can be sold. This is normally done at the County Clerk's office. You will be asked to provide a copy of the will, if there is one, and death certificate or other documents depending on your situation.

The amount of time probating a will takes will depend on the workload of the office you are filing your probate with. It could take anywhere between 2 weeks to several months. If you are told the process should take quite a while, talk with your attorney about your situation concerning the sale of property.

Getting this resolved before you have a purchase agreement will prevent headaches and frustration in meeting the contract deadlines and fulfilling the probation requirements.

See Page 87 For Your Free Service Offer

If there is more than one heir to the estate all parties should have their names on the purchase contract as a seller and will also need to sign closing documents. The attorney handling the probate will be able to advise you on how the ownership on the purchase contract should be written.

The Mortgage Process

When you are considering an offer on your home you will want the lender's contact information to make sure the buyer is qualified to purchase your home. Due to privacy laws the lender ca not give you information about their credit scores or any other confidential information without the buyer's approval. However, you should be able to find out if the buyer is eligible for a loan.

In the event the buyer has representation by an agent, you should contact the agent for this information. You will want to find out:

- Has the lender received a copy of the receipted contract? They should receive this from the buyer or their agent. Whatever the situation is you need to confirm the lender have a legible copy. If they don't have one, get them a copy. The lender can't start working on the loan process until they receive a signed contract.

- After the option period is up you will want to contact the lender or agent to see when the appraisal will be in and if there are any issues that you need to address concerning the home. What you want to be concerned with here is; are there any repairs you are unaware of they will insist on being done before funding will take place. Major repairs would consist of repairs to the foundation, roof, plumbing or septic system if there is one.

- If a survey needs to be ordered you will want to find out when they intend to order one. This is normally done the week before closing. In some states surveys are transferable. If your survey is transferable you need to make sure both the lender and title company have a copy and find out when you can expect approval by the underwriters.

In the financial portion of the contract will be a date or number of days before the lender will give final approval. In most cases it will take the lender 21-30 days to do this. It simply has to do with their process.

During the option period the lender will be collecting all the information they need from the buyer and confirming their documentation. After the option period the lender will order an appraisal; this could take up to 7 days. Once the appraisal is in and the survey has been approved everything then goes to the underwriter.

Be aware that if any documents are missing or the underwriter wants more information they will not give approval until the necessary documents are received. Once the underwriter has everything that they need it should only take 48 – 72 hours for final approval.

After final approval has been given the lender will send closing instructions to the title company. When the lender has approved the HUD 1 Statement, all parties will sign the closing documents.

The Option Period & Home Inspections

During the option period, the buyer will have offered you an amount of money for a set number of days to have the home inspected. This money should be given to you upon agreement of the contract. The check should be made out to you, the seller. The money for this option period is yours to keep whether the buyer decides to cancel the contract during their option period or not. If they move forward with the purchase after the home inspections, the option money will be reflected on the closing HUD 1 Statement as a credit to you that the buyer has already paid you the option money.

The buyer should schedule, pay for the inspection, and be with the inspector of their choice. It will be your responsibility to have all the utilities turned on so the inspection can be done. You will also want to make sure the buyer has a copy of your seller's disclosure to insure the buyer and their inspectors have all the information they need.

<u>This option period time is for the buyer to decide if they want to purchase the home or not</u>. Be aware that during this time they may want to renegotiate the price or request repairs upon reviewing the home inspections.

See Page 87 For Your Free Service Offer

Several different types of home inspections could be done on the home depending on where the property is located and its condition.

Here is a list of the most common inspections. This will give you an indication on what to expect but is not limited to only these types of inspections.

- Home Inspection
- Septic Inspection
- Well Water Testing
- Energy Audit
- Foundation Inspection
- Roof Inspection

Home Inspection

The home inspection will give the buyer a general overview of the current condition of your home. These are the basics that the inspector will check, however, each inspector may do thing a little differently.

- Air Conditioner & Heating Unit - This will involve checking the airflow, filter, coils, & drain system. Both the interior & exterior units will be observed.

- Appliances – They will turn on the stove checking for temperature settings and that all burners work properly. The dishwasher will be run through a complete cycle. If there is a built in microwave they will check the working order of this appliance also, along with the garbage disposal should there be one.

- Electrical – All light switches and electrical outlets will be tested. They will look at the breaker box and any exposed wiring of these breakers or outlets.

- Plumbing – All drains will be stopped up, water will be run, and the drains will be released. They will be looking for dripping faucets and slow or clogged drains. They will look for any evidence of water leaks under the sinks and around the home. Exterior faucets will also be checked.

- The roof and attic - This will include the structure type, insulation, and the shingles or roof covering. Any roof damage will be noted in their report.

- Foundation – The inspector will note any visible cracks or sloping in the foundation, by

See Page 87 For Your Free Service Offer

observing exterior portions of the home and interior walls and flooring.

- Doors & Windows – All doors and windows will be opened and closed to make sure they work property. This includes the garage door.

The home inspector may also inspect for termites and wood destroying insects however, this may require a separate inspector. The same is true for wells and septic systems if you have them.

In the event there are any issues the inspector addresses that the buyer is concerned with, the buyer may choose to have other inspections done. In most cases it will be concerning the roof, plumbing, foundation, electrical, air conditioning or heating units. If this arises you may want to consider allowing the buyer more time for further inspection should they need it.

The roof, electrical, foundation & plumbing are major issues and could be something that would prevent the lender from financing the home loan.

Other Inspections

Wells - The same inspector that inspected the home may be licensed to test the water depending on the area you live in. Some areas may require a separate inspector from the city, county, or MUD; or a water sample may need to be sent to a testing facility.

Septic Systems – It is in your best interest to disclose everything you know about the septic system to the buyer. The septic system will need to be pumped and inspected. This normally will be done by a licensed septic inspector. Depending on where you live this may need to be done by someone within your governing water district, or by a company that is licensed to install and service septic systems.

Who pays to have the septic system uncovered and pumped should be determined in the contract before inspections begin. The fee for uncovering the lid and having the system pumped should not include the fee for having the system inspected – unless one of you has agreed to pay the full expense of this inspection.

Energy Audits – Some cities are trying to go green and now requiring an energy audit be done on your home when you sell it. Check with your city or local utility company to see if one of these needs to be done or not. If so, there may be policies exempting your home from this type of inspection. Such items might be: have you participated in any local energy efficient programs, if the home is less than 10 years old, if it's investment property or not, the location may also be a deciding factor.

You and the buyer will need to determine who pays for such inspections; this should be put in writing in the purchase agreement. It is also wise to have any and all necessary inspections done during the time allotted for the option period.

Negotiating Repairs

After all the inspections are done the buyer may come to you with a list of repairs they would like you to complete. If they have a realtor it will come on an Amendment or Addendum form. If not, be sure to put everything in writing that you agree to and all parties' involved need to sign it. This should be added to your purchase agreement and become part of your contract. This will prevent any future misunderstandings.

If the buyer or their agent, request any repairs, as a courtesy you should get a copy of the inspection report; if not ask for one. The inspector's name and phone number should be on the report. If not, ask for it. You may have questions concerning what exactly the inspector is referring to. The inspector will talk with you and answer any questions you have about the report.

See Page 87 For Your Free Service Offer

When negotiating repairs keep in mind that you don't have to do any repairs except what the lender may require. If there are major issues that need to be addressed fix them. If you can't afford to do so, many companies will do the repairs and send the invoice to the title company to be paid on the closing day once they know you have a purchase contract and the closing date. You will also need to provide the closers contact information for them. The repair amount will be deducted from your profits and be reflected on the HUD 1 Statement as an expense to you.

You will also want to contact the lender to make sure everything is still good on the buyers end. Be careful not to put yourself in a situation where you're stuck with expensive home repairs if the buyer has financing issues they still need to work on for the lender. Carefully consider all your options taking into account what repairs you are willing to make.

Instead of making small repairs you could renegotiate the sale price. If a price reduction is agreed to get it in writing, have all parties sign and date it. A copy of this change will need to go to the lender and closing company. <u>Not notifying the lender of any financial adjustments could delay your closing</u>.

Home Service Agreements

A Home Service Agreement is something that can be purchased by either the buyer or seller for a piece of residential real estate. There is an annual fee. It covers items like, the dishwasher, garbage disposal, hot water heater, and garage door openers. Some policies cover wood destroying insect issues and the pump to the pool or hot tub. Should anything like this break once the new home owner has moved in, the Service Agreement should cover most of those expenses.

You may be asked to pay for the initial purchase of such a Service Agreement. Should you choose to do so, you need to know:

- There are a variety of packages available. The average annual fee ranges between $350.00 - $500.00
- Home Service Agreements are for one year at a time.
- If you currently have one on the property, it may be transferable to the new owner.
- Add-ons to the Service Agreement can cover things like the septic, pool, hot tub, or even termites.

Should you agree to pay for this, the amount filled into the contract is the limit upon which you can be charged. If the buyer wants more then what

See Page 87 For Your Free Service Offer

you agreed to pay, the balance is their expense and the difference will be included in their closing cost on the HUD 1 Statement.

Depending on the other agreements in the contract you may decide not to pay for this. If so, know that the buyer can still obtain this at his or her own expense. It can even be added as an addendum to their home owner's insurance. If you have a newer home you may consider saying no. If you have an older home you may agree to pick up the expense or split the cost.

Providing the new owner with a one-year Home Service Agreement is a small price to pay, to ensure you have done everything possible to protect yourself from any repercussions; should an appliance break one month after the new owner moves in.

Home Owners Associations & Documents

If you live in a community that has a Home Owners Association the buyer has the right to receive a copy of the Resale Certificate, Rules and Regulations, and By-Laws. It is the seller's responsibility to provide this to the buyer. Here is another loophole and how you need to tighten it up.

The amount of time for the buyer to review the Home Owners Association documents should reflect the same number of days as the option period, or very close to it. And this is why! In most contracts it allows an allotted period of time for you to get the documents to the buyer and a separate time frame for their review.

Example: Say you have a 5-day option period and a 14-day time frame concerning the HOA documents. On day 8 you deliver the HOA docs to the buyer. The buyer still has 6 more days to review the documents and object to anything in the Home Owners Association documents.

By now you may be wondering what they could object to. Let's suppose the HOA documents reflect something like - you can't have a home-based business. If the buyer works part-time from their home as a CPA during the tax season that is an out for the buyer. **The buyer can object to anything in the Home Owners Association documents**

See Page 87 For Your Free Service Offer

and walk away within the number of days allowed according to the contract.

The more time the buyer has to object to anything in the Home Owners Association documents, the longer your home will be off the market should they decide to walk away.

The Appraisal

An appraisal is required by the lender on any property that is being financed. This is to protect the buyer from paying too much and the lender from financing a property that is priced above the markets value. If you have a contract that reflects an option period, in most cases, the lender will not order the appraisal until that time frame is up.

Once the appraisal has been ordered it could take up to 5-7 days for the appraiser to inspect the property and complete the report. The appraiser then sends a copy of the appraisal to both the buyer and lender for their review.

What if the appraisal comes in lower than the purchase price?

The lender will not finance a piece of property with an appraised value lower than the purchase offer. If this is your situation three things can happen at this point.

1. The seller needs to come down on the price to match the appraised value.
2. The buyer will need to bring the difference to the closing.
3. The lender will not finance the loan for more than the appraised value and the buyer gets to walk away.

See Page 87 For Your Free Service Offer

What if there are issues with the appraisal?

Lenders will not fund a home that has foundation problems; major plumbing or electrical problems; or in need of a new roof until these problems are repaired. From an investing point of view lenders will not finance anything that is in need of major repairs – it simply is not a good investment.

If any of these issues come up - the buyer, their agent, or the lender should contact you concerning what needs to be repaired.

1. Something will need to be put in writing stating that you will correct the problem. This documentation will need to be signed by all parties and given to the lender and closer with the title company.

2. The repairs will need to be done before the closing.

3. Receipts of these repairs will need to be sent to the lender before the underwriter will give final approval.

See Page 87 For Your Free Service Offer

If repairs are needed it is wiser for you to pay a professional company to make these repairs instead of you doing them, even if you work in that profession. This way you are not held liable should anything come up concerning these repairs in the future.

To avoid this situation simply have your home inspected by a licensed inspector before you market your home for sale so you can make the repairs ahead of time or at least know what to expect.

The Survey

In some states surveys are transferable between buyer and seller as long as no changes have been made to the current survey. There may be certain requirements that may need to be met before this can take place. This could be the signing of an affidavit stating there has been no change, there may be a survey age limit, or has it been transferred before. The buyer, the title company, and the lender also must accept a previous survey.

If your buyer has a real estate agent that is using their standard real estate promulgated forms, there will be a paragraph that discusses this and it should be negotiable. If it is negotiable your options are: The buyer or seller can pay for a new one or the current one may be transferred.

If you do have a transferable survey you will need to get it to the title company and sign an affidavit concerning the survey. This affidavit will need to be notarized and can be done at the title company when you drop off the survey. A copy of the survey and affidavit will also need to go to the buyer and lender for their approval.

If you live in another town or state from the property you are selling, ask that the affidavit be sent to you for your signature and send it back along with the survey for acceptance. In most cases the

See Page 87 For Your Free Service Offer

affidavit is a standard form and can be emailed to you for a faster response.

The title company will need to submit the survey and affidavit to their underwriters for final approval. In most cases if the title company approves the survey so will the lender.

If any changes have been made to the property since you have owned the property you may want to strongly consider having another one purchased at either the buyer's or your expense, depending on the terms of you contract.

Changes that the underwriter will be looking for on the survey have to do with the exterior portion of the property or landlines. Such as: adding or removing a deck or pool; adding, replacing or moving a fence; adding a workshop, storage building, or room onto a house. This is just an example of some of the changes but not all that could have occurred while you have owned the property.

If you accepted the previous owner's survey it is in your best interest to have a new one done. Let me explain why. This is simply a scenario of what could happen.

Let's say you purchased a home 5 years ago and the survey was transferred to you at that time.

See Page 87 For Your Free Service Offer

Now you are selling your home and you are transferring the survey again. The new owner wants to replace the fence and in doing so finds out that part of his property is in the neighbor's back yard. According to the neighbor the first owner had put the fence up himself. Let's take it a little further and say the neighbor had planted some trees along the fence line in his back yard and now those trees are 9 years old. It would be very expensive to have them moved not to mention an upset neighbor. Then you still have the main problem with the neighbor having possession of land that doesn't belong to him.

I'm sure you can see where this is headed…. The new owner may be looking to you for a solution to the problem. It is in <u>your</u> best interest for a new survey done no matter who pays for that expense.

If you don't have a transferable survey a new one will need to be ordered. If this is the case the title company will order this before closing and the fees for the survey will be added to the HUD 1 Statement at closing. In most cases the title company will not order the survey until the buyer's lender tells them to do so. This is normally done the week before the closing date. The expense of a new survey is negotiable and can be paid for by the buyer or seller.

See Page 87 For Your Free Service Offer

The Title Commitment

The title company needs to receive the escrow money and the contract. They will sign the receipted part of the contract to confirm that they have accepted the buyer's earnest money check. The earnest money check needs to be made out to the title company.

When you deliver the contract and earnest money to the title company you can drop off the survey and sign their affidavit concerning the survey, should you have a transferable survey. If you have chosen to transfer your current survey to the new owner, the title company's underwriter will review the survey and affidavit. They will need to give their approval before the survey can be transferred to the new owner. If the title company approves the survey a copy of the survey and affidavit will need to be sent to the buyer and their lender for approval. This will normally be done by the title company.

Within 5 – 10 working days you will receive a Title Commitment from the title company concerning the sale of your property for your review. In the top right corner on most of these pages you will find a G.F. Number. This is the file number used by the title company for this transaction. Have this number close by when you call the title company for updates. On occasion your closer may be unable to take your call

See Page 87 For Your Free Service Offer

and the receptionist or their assistant may ask you for this number.

Schedules A, B and C

When you receive the title commitment, you will need to review Schedules A, B and C.

Schedule A has to do with the sale price, the loan amount, type of deed, who holds the deed and the legal description.

Schedule B normally has to do with easements, right of ways, mineral or water rights and things of this nature.

Schedule C normally will address the liens on the property. Pay special attention here. Sometimes there will be errors. All debts and liens against your property must be paid at closing or cleared up before a clear title to the property can be issued.

The title company will take care of any erroneous issues for you but will need your help in doing so. They may ask you for documents or information that you will need to provide. This will enable them to take care of these maters on your behalf. Below are some examples of what may appear in your Title Commitment.

One common error would be if you have a last name like: Miller, Smith, Jones, or Garcia. There are

See Page 87 For Your Free Service Offer

a lot of people with these last names. If your name is Mary A. Jones, the "A" could be for Ann, Ana, Angela, or Angie.

Giving the closer your social security number so they can have incorrect names removed can easily clear up this situation. You may also be asked to sign a form stating you are not these other people.

Other reasons could be someone has filed a lien against your property other than the mortgage note. Some of these could be:

- A Mechanic's Lien – This is for outstanding services rendered.

- A Judgment – This is a court ordered settlement.

- Old Outstanding Debts – You may not even be aware that there are any other liens on your home other than the mortgage note, a second lien, or a home improvement loan.

- Tax Liens or Home Owners Association Fees.

If there are erroneous liens on your property, these issues can be cleared from the title commitment. If any issue shows up you have already taken care of, the title company will tell you what documents they need according to the specific situation to clear it off the Title Commitment. Sometimes it's as simple as the proper documents were never filed at the county clerk's office to clear a lien from your property.

If something shows up that still needs to be paid. That can be taken care of at closing from the proceeds of the sale of the property.

Married or Divorced Since the Property Was Purchased

Here are some things you need to know if you have been married or divorced since the purchase of the property.

If you have been married since you purchased the property, your new spouse may need to sign a document pertaining to the property. It will basically say that they are your partner and they are aware you are selling the property. If you had a prenuptial agreement stating that this property is separate from your joint properties, you may need to provide the prenuptial agreement to the closer. Check with your Title Company or Attorney concerning the laws in your state. Depending on the laws, your spouse's name may need to be on the contract or they may be asked to attend the closing.

See Page 87 For Your Free Service Offer

If you have been divorced since you purchased the property have a notarized copy of your Divorce Decree available. You will be asked for a copy, especially if your ex-spouse's name has shown up on the title. If your ex-spouse is due any portion of the profits from the sale of the property, the Title Company will make arrangements for them to receive their portion. Some documents may also need to be signed by this person depending on your states laws.

If your ex-spouse has moved away you will need to provide contact information for this person. If this person needs to sign any documents; the closer can FedEx the documents to the ex-spouse and wire their portion of the proceeds into their bank account should any be due them.

Depending on your situation they may also need to sign and agree to all the terms of the contract. Consult with an attorney concerning your specific situation if you are unsure.

If you don't have a copy of your Divorce Decree you can obtain a copy from the County Clerk's Office in which your divorce became legal. There will be a small fee to the County Clerk's Office for a notarized copy of the Decree.

Wills, Probates, and Death Certificates

If you are the Executor of an Estate the property you are selling will need to have been probated before the property can be sold. The time it will take for the property to be probated will depend on your Attorney and the Probate Department. It could take a few weeks or up to several months, each situation is different. You're Attorney, or the Probate Department will advise you on what is needed and the length of time to expect before the property can be sold.

This does not mean that you can't accept a purchase offer on the property. It simply means the sale can't be completed until everything has been recorded with the County's Probate Department.

In the event a spouse has passed on since the purchase of your home and their name appears on the title, you may need to present a copy of the Death Certificate. You may also be asked for a copy of the Will or Trust if there is one.

If there are any other parties that may have an interest in the property they will need to be notified. Their names may need to be added to the contract or they may need to sign closing documents depending on the terms of the Will or Trust. The title company will disburse the funds from the sale of the property to all parties as instructed in the Will or Trust.

If one or more of the heirs live in another city or state, the title company can have the documents sent to that person. The documents will be sent by using an over-night courier service like FedEx. This person then signs the documents and returns them to the Title Company. This process should not take longer than 24-48 hours.

Another alternative is for the heir that is unable to attend the closing to give someone Power of Attorney to sign on their behalf. The Title Company or Attorney's Office will have a form they can sign, have witnessed and notarized, then given to the closer before final documents are signed. The Title Company will need the original Power of Attorney. In most cases the Title Company will provide this service free of charge.

If any of these situations apply to you, consult with your Attorney or the Title Company where you intend to finalize the sale of the property. They will be able to answer all your questions and let you know what documents you need to provide before the final documents are signed.

Property Taxes and Home Owners Association Dues

Property taxes and Home Owner Association dues will be prorated and the amounts will be reflected on your HUD 1 Statement at the closing. Property taxes are prorated through the day of closing and most Home Owners Association dues are prorated by the month. Any delinquent taxes or dues will be deducted at the closing and be on the HUD 1 Statement.

A more detailed explanation will be in the next Chapter - Closing Day under the subheading HUD 1 Statement.

Closing Day

When closing day approaches there are several things you need to know and take with you to the closing. This will prevent any delays in receiving the profits from the sale of the property.

About five to seven days before everyone is to sign the closing documents you will need to schedule a closing time with the Title Company. The appointment will need to be set for the day you and the buyer agreed to in your contract. This may change if the loan documents are not complete.

If the loan documents are not complete it may back up your closing a few days. Just be aware, this is a normal occurrence. Should this happen, in most probability this has nothing to do with the buyer's qualifications it is normally caused by the lenders workload or them not receiving the numerous documents they need within the time frame they requested; such as the appraisal or survey.

The lender will be sending the loan documents to their underwriter for final approval usually 3 – 4 days before the closing day. You will want to check in with the buyer or their agent to see when this is being done and when they expect to receive final approval. You will also need to find out what time the buyer intends to sign their closing documents. If you both feel comfortable with it, you can both sign your closing documents at the same time.

Since you are the seller you will not have a lot of closing documents to sign. You should plan on being there approximately one hour and will need to take two forms of identification. One will need to be a current photo ID - like a state issued driver's license; a Social Security card, Passport, or Military ID should be acceptable as the second form of identification.

If you have any warranties concerning the property either for work that has been done or any appliances you may be leaving with the property, take those with you. Also include all keys and the garage door openers. You can just put them all in a large envelope and give them to the closer. The closer should not give the buyer these items before the mortgage lender has wired the money to the Title Company; unless you tell the closer differently.

Tenants

If you have tenants living in the property for sale, most likely the buyer has already asked to see a copy of the lease or asked for detailed information about this agreement. At the closing you will need to provide the original lease agreements and the tenant's contact information.

See Page 87 For Your Free Service Offer

Before the closing you will need to notify the tenants there will be a new owner and give them contact information on the buyer. This removes you from any further obligation to the tenants once the closing documents have been signed.

You will also need to give the buyer a check for the tenants deposit and the rent will need to be prorated if you are not signing documents on the day the rent is due. All deposits are transferable to the buyer at closing unless otherwise agreed to in the written terms of the contract.

Seller Temporary Lease

In some states you are expected to be moved out the day you sign the closing documents. Should you live in the home you are selling, you may need or want a few extra days to move out, after the final documents have been signed. If this is the case you may need to have a Temporary Lease Agreement signed by all parties and a move out date agreed to.

In this event you will need to present a check to the buyer for the deposit and lease amount agreed to. You should have two separate checks. One should be for the deposit and the other for the rent amount. If the lease back is only for a few days the buyer my just hold your deposit check and return it to you once you have moved out and they have inspected the home for any damages that may have occurred during the new ownership.

The buyer will also need to let you know who to make the checks out to. If they are investors and doing business under a company name they may want you to make the checks out to the company and not them personally.

If you are doing a Temporary Lease you will still need to give the buyer a set of keys to the property. They will be the new owner, you will be their tenant, and legally they have a right to a set of keys to the property.

Buyer Temporary Lease

On occasion a buyer may need to move in early. If the property is vacant you may consider this option. The most common reasons for a buyer asking for a Temporary Lease are:

- They need to move out of their current location before the close date due to the sale of their home.
- Their lease may be up.
- They may be temporarily living in a hotel due to their company relocating them.

If the property is currently vacant, and you feel comfortable with the buyer moving in early, you will need to have them sign a Temporary Lease Agreement. The buyer will need to give you a deposit and a rent amount. You will need to receive these checks before the buyer moves in. If the closing is delayed a few days due to the lenders documents not being ready, it will be your responsibility to collect additional rent money from them.

The HUD 1 Statement

A HUD 1 Statement is a form that is required by the U.S. Department of Housing and Urban Development on all Real Estate or Mortgage transactions. All Real Estate Closers, throughout the United States, must use this form. It is also referred to as a Closing Statement or Settlement Sheet. The purpose of this form is to itemize all the financials concerning the transaction.

The government requires that the HUD 1 Statement be filled out by a neutral party. Meaning – no one with any vested interest in the property can fill in the form. This results in the neutral party being an entity like a Title Company or Real Estate Attorney's Office.

Before all parties can sign the HUD 1 Statement, there are several things that need to occur. Once the lender's underwriter gives final approval, they will prepare loan documents that are sent to the closing company. When the closer receives the loan documents they prepare the HUD 1 Statement.

The HUD 1 Statement will reflect all charges, expenses and credits to both the buyer and the seller. In some states two separate HUD 1 Statements are prepared, one for the seller's signature and the other for the buyer's. These items will include the escrow deposit, taxes, loan fees, insurance, repair invoices, purchase amount, recording fees and any transfer fees.

After the finances are calculated and placed on the form the closer sends the HUD 1 Statement back to the lender for their review and approval. At this time both the seller and the buyer and any agents involved should receive a copy for review. This is normally referred to as the first draft. It is highly important that everything on this document be accurate. Once all parties have signed the Closing Statement the transaction is considered complete and no revisions should need to be made.

If you have any questions about the HUD 1 Statement the closer will be happy to answer them for you. If you notice an error on the statement let the closer know right away so they can make the necessary changes.

On behalf of the seller, the closer will see to it any liens on the property are paid off upon receiving funding from the lender. If you have any mortgages, or home improvement loans the closer will ask you for the loan number, the company name, and your social security number. They will call the lender that currently hold your note and ask for the payoff amount. This is done a day or two before the closing and the amount will be included on the Closing Statement.

Property Taxes and HOA Calculations

Property Taxes will be prorated through the day of closing. The calculated portion of the taxes that are your responsibility will be deducted from the profits of the sale and credited to the buyer on the HUD 1 Statement. It will then be the buyer's responsibility to pay the property taxes when they become due within your state.

The property taxes are calculated by a daily amount. Then the daily amount is multiplied by how many days there have been in the tax period – including the day everyone signs the final documents.

If there are any delinquent taxes the Title Company will deduct the amount due from your proceeds and make sure they are paid to the taxing authorities. The Title Company is responsible for

See Page 87 For Your Free Service Offer

clearing all liens on the property and issuing the buyer a clear title to the property.

The Home Owners Association Dues are also prorated. Should there be any past due amounts the closer will deduct that amount from your profits and pay the Home Owners Association.

When the Title Company contacts the Home Owners Association for information on current or back dues, they normally notify the Home Owners Association of a pending sale. This is usually done a few days before closing.

Title Companies or Attorney's Office should take care of this for you. If you have any doubts that this may not be done, feel free to follow up with the Home Owners Association to make sure they have received all the information needed.

After the Documents Are Signed

Once all parties to the transaction have signed all the documents, you will receive a copy of the signed HUD 1 Statement. You will want to keep this document. There is information on this form that can be used for tax purposes. It is also your documentation concerning payment of property taxes and Home Owners Association fees.

After the signing of the documents the closer will contact the lender to let them know everything

See Page 87 For Your Free Service Offer

has been completed. The lender will then wire money to the title company. At that time the title company will disburse all money concerning the sale. This is when you will receive your portion.

There are two ways you can receive your money. They can cut you a Cashier's Check or they can wire the money directly into a bank account of your choosing. To wire the money the closer will need the routing number and an account number. The closer may ask for a deposit slip or voided check with the routing number printed on it.

Even though looking at the large dollar amount on a check made out to you is fun, you may be disappointed when you go to deposit the check and find out the bank intends to hold the check for a few of days. This amount of time could be as much as 7 – 10 days. In most cases, when money is wired directly into your account, you have immediate access to your money. Check with your bank on their policy before you make that decision. It would be a shame if you were planning an immediate move or trip and could not access the money you may need right away.

Out of Town Closings

On occasion the buyer or seller may live in another town or state from the property, need to move before the closing, or will be out of town on

See Page 87 For Your Free Service Offer

business the day the closing is scheduled. There are a few options to consider.

- The closing company can use an overnight courier service like FedEx to send the documents. Companies such as these do not deliver to P.O. Boxes so a physical address will be required. In the documents that will be sent there should be a prepaid return envelope and instructions on everything that needs to be done concerning the documents.

- Another option would be to have someone else sign the documents for you by using a Power of Attorney. In this case the Power of Attorney that the Title Company or Attorney's Offices use should be specific to that transaction only. These offices will have one that can be signed before the closing. The form will need to be witnessed and signed by a notary, which can be completed in their office.

Manufactured and Modular Homes

If you own a Manufactured or Modular home it may very well be that you have a title to the home and a deed for the land. All manufactured, modular, and mobile homes are considered personal property and you will have a separate title for this type of home. It is similar to an automobile title. They are considered personal property simply because they can be moved. The land is considered real estate.

If you own the land and home both they can be combined into one unit of real estate. The title company will take care of the paperwork on this for you. However, there will be things you, as the seller will need to do. The buyer's lender will require some of these things.

- You will need to surrender both the title to the home and deed to the land.
- The manufactured home will need to be enclosed around the bottom. You may also be required to install insulation underneath the home. Allow for a crawl space under the home should any future repairs need to be made.
- If the tongue (for moving purposed) has not been removed you will need to have it removed.
- Metal cables connecting the home to the land will need to be secured under the home. They

will need to be welded to the cross beams and anchored into the ground with cement.

The lender, inspector or appraiser will let you know what specifications are required to satisfy the lender for loan approval. These things will need to be taken care of before the lender will approve financing. Once their requirements have been met, the land and home can be merged together as one property and considered real estate.

If this was done before you owned the property. There may be only a few minor adjustments that need to be done to satisfy the lenders specifications.

Financially Distressed Properties: Foreclosures & Short Sales

Losses of employment or medical crises are the two main reasons for home foreclosure. Either one of these situations could leave anyone in a financially stressed situation. If you have found yourself in a pre-foreclosure situation you may be considering selling your home yourself simply because you can't afford to pay a Realtor's commission. Should you be in this situation know you have options to consider.

1. Bringing the loan current is the most favorable option with your mortgage lender. If there is reasonable expectation of income in the near future, that will be enough where you could maintain the mortgage note, it may be to your advantage to discuss a short-term loan even if that means asking a friend or family member.

2. Forbearance is another option to consider. This is where the mortgage lender allows you to reduce and spread the missed payments out over a period of a few months, allowing you to get caught up. Be sure to read the agreement carefully, weighing the pros and cons. Some agreements state that the lender can immediately foreclose on you if you fall behind

See Page 87 For Your Free Service Offer

on your payments ever again. Keep in mind that your current payments are still due along with the payment arrangements you make for the past due amount.

3. The Loan Modification is when the lender agrees to reduce the principal, interest or monthly payment. Normally this is done through the Loss Mitigation Department with your lending company.

4. A Short Sale is when the lender allows you to sell your home for a reduced amount than what you currently owe on the home. If this is agreed to – all the money from the sale will go directly to the lender. The homeowner is not allowed to profit from the sale. A short sale will prevent you from purchasing another home for at least two years.

5. Foreclosure is when the lender goes through the process of having you evicted and taking the home back. A foreclosure will drop your credit score 200 – 300 points and could prevent you from purchasing another home for seven years or longer.

See Page 87 For Your Free Service Offer

The Foreclosure Process

Both the short sale and foreclosure process are expensive and time consuming for the lender. Dealing with the Loss Mitigation Department of your lender will be slow and at times even down right frustrating. Expect to be on hold for long periods of time or being transferred throughout the phone conversations.

Every time you are in contact with the lender be prepared to give them your account number and your social security number. When communicating through any form of written correspondence include your account number and name on each page. <u>If the lender asks you to fax any documents – be sure to include your name and account number in the margin at both the bottom and top of each page.</u>

When you fall behind on your mortgage payments the lender starts the foreclosure process by first sending you late notices. Depending on the lender and your states laws this could be anywhere between 1 – 5 notices. If you have fallen behind on your mortgage note, it is in your best interest to respond to these notices when you start receiving them in the mail.

The second step the lender will take will be to order a Notice of Default from the County Clerk's Office. This is a formal notice that legal action is

See Page 87 For Your Free Service Offer

being taken and the foreclosure process has begun. If you have not already made contact with the person sending the notices, and you intend to try and keep your home, it is in your best interest to contact the Loss Mitigation Office that has sent the notice. Contact information should be stated in the letters you have been receiving. If not, look at the letterhead for a phone number and ask for the person that signed the letter.

When you are speaking with the lender about your situation, keep in mind they are human too and they are there to help you the best they can within the parameters of the laws they have to adhere to. The person you speak with could have hundreds of accounts in their portfolio so be kind. They will appreciate your cooperation and work with you as effectively as they can.

The amount of time you have will depend upon the State and County in which you live. Once you receive the Notice of Default you will have a set amount of time to move out. If the notice does not state how long you have, contact the office issuing the statement of eviction. If you do not move out of the home by the designated date the County Sherriff can be given authority to remove the residents from the home.

See Page 87 For Your Free Service Offer

Please note – each State and County are different on the amount of time you are allowed to move. The time you are given could be as little as 21 days depending on the laws in your area.

If you are approaching foreclosure you may want to seek the counsel of a real estate attorney in your area to get more specific information. They will be familiar with housing and foreclosure laws in your area and counsel you on your situation.

The next notice will be the Notice of Sale; this notice will be posted on the property. A time and location for the sale of foreclosed property should be on the Notice for Sale. At the sell, the property will be auctioned off to the public, to the highest bidder. If you are to this point and you still want your home seek the advice of a real estate attorney to see if you are eligible to make a bid at the auction.

Once the property is Real Estate Owned or Bank Owned, the new deed will be recorded and the property will be listed for sale by the bank through a Realtor.

Some states have a redemption period where the previous owner has a specific amount of time to clear up the default. Some states will even allow you to remain in the property during this redemption period. If your state does not have a redemption period, and you are still living in the home, expect to be evicted.

A foreclosure will affect your credit score by 200 – 300 points and will prevent you from purchasing another home for 7 years.

Short Sales

When a homeowner is in a pre-foreclosure situation a Short Sale is an option to discuss with the Mortgage Lender. A short sale is when a lender will accept a lesser amount than the loan balance when the owner is selling their home. The lender does not have to agree to a short sale but should be taken into consideration. They will also need to approve the sale amount.

You may be asking yourself; why would a mortgage lender do this? Mortgage lenders are in the business of loaning money not in selling or maintaining real estate. The foreclosure process is also very expensive.

The advantage to you for selling your home through a short sale is it will be less devastating to your credit report. This way will allow you to recover from the set back and strengthen your credit score, enabling you to purchase another home within a few years, depending on how quickly you recover.

See Page 87 For Your Free Service Offer

Should you decide to discuss the short sale option with your lender there are a few things you need to know.

- The homeowner is not allowed to financially benefit from the sale of the property.

- The homeowner is not normally allowed to live in the house after the transaction is complete.

- The IRS could consider debt forgiveness as taxable income. The homeowner should fill out the correct tax forms to request tax forgiveness from the government. Your CPA will be able to advise and assist you with the correct documents for this situation.

- There is no guarantee that the lender who accepts a short sale will not legally pursue you for the balance between the sale amount received and the remaining portion of your loan. Do your best to negotiate with the lender to accept the offer and not pursuing you for the balance after the sale.

The same holds true concerning a Short Sale as it does with a Foreclosure. When contacting the Loss Mitigation Department with your lender, you will be asked for your account number and social security

See Page 87 For Your Free Service Offer

number. You can expect to be put on hold and transferred to different people. Keep notes on who you talked to, what was discussed, the date and time.

If the lender agrees you are eligible for a short sale you will need a Short Sale Package. Below is a basic list of forms or information you will be asked for. Some lenders may require more information.

- Hardship Letter.
- Financial Worksheet.
- Copies of Tax Returns – the last 2 years from all borrowers.
- Copies of All Bank Statements – normally the last 2 months from all borrowers.
- Copies of Pay Stubs – from all borrowers.
- Listing Agreement.
- Authorization to Release Information Form – this is necessary for your Realtor to speak with the Lender.
- Purchase Offer – if there is one.

The hardship letter will need to include an explanation of your hardship. Loss of income could be anyone who is a main contributor to the mortgage note and their name should be on the mortgage note. If you have been laid off, your lender may want documentation from your previous employer.

See Page 87 For Your Free Service Offer

In a situation where a spouse dies and was an income provider, this too could be considered loss of income. In this situation a death certificate will be needed.

A serious illness would be considered if there is reduced income due to a lengthy medical condition or hospital stays, or excessive missed work due to medical rehabilitation.

The lender will provide the **Authorization to Release Information Form** for your signature. If you have a Realtor, include their name and contact information. If they have an assistant include their name and contact information also. The lenders are very strict with this and will not speak to anyone concerning this situation other than the owner unless their name is on this form. This has to do with privacy laws to protect the consumer.

If you have a written **purchase contract** at the time you are applying for a Short Sale include it when returning the short sale package. This will increase your chances of a short sale being accepted.

<u>Also be aware that your lenders agreement to a Short Sale does not always stop their foreclosure process. The foreclosure attorney will still be moving forward with this process. Time is crucial.</u>

See Page 87 For Your Free Service Offer

Keep in mind when sending any documents to the lender to include your name and account number at the top and bottom of each page. Some lenders will have you fax the forms in. Some fax machines will resize the documents cutting off a portion of the document at the top or bottom of each page. By putting your account number and name at both the top and bottom of each page helps prevent documents from being misplaced once they are received.

It is your responsibility to follow up with your lender and make sure they have received all the documents. Once the bank receives all the short sale documents, they may change the terms of the purchase offer or sale price.

- Once the lender receives the completed short sale package the process could take up to a few months for finalization of the properties sale.
- Your lender will want to know the current value of the property before they accept any purchase offer. They will order their own appraisal of the property. Once the appraisal is ordered it could take a few weeks before the lender gives you an answer on the purchase offer.
- Lenders will not agree to make any repairs. The buyer is purchasing the home "As-Is".

See Page 87 For Your Free Service Offer

- In most cases the lender will not contribute any money to the buyers closing cost.

Being able to present a purchase offer along with all the other information will greatly increase your chances of having a short sale accepted by your lender. The simpler and less complicated the offer is, combined with a fair purchase price, the more likely the purchase offer will be accepted by your lender.

If you have tried everything you know to do and still had no luck finding a buyer it is time to consider listing your home with a Realtor. If you do not have the property listed for sale with a Realtor and the lender agrees to a short sell the lender may insist on you finding a real estate agent to list your property. The clock is ticking and time is of the essence.

Let me explain how most realtors get paid. When you list your property for sale with a Realtor, in most cases, they work on a commission basis. The percentage of commission will vary depending on where you live. Know that this amount is negotiable. This commission is also split between the real estate company that list your home and the company that brings the buyer. Some Realtors will reduce their commission if you ask and some will work for a flat fee. The Realtor's commission will be paid at closing after all parties have signed the closing documents.

See Page 87 For Your Free Service Offer

Should you already have the property listed for sell with a realtor the commission agreed to on the original listing agreement may change once the bank accepts your short sale package. The bank will determine this depending on how much debt you have against the loan, how much the closing fees are and what the purchase price is.

When interviewing a realtor it would be wise to find out how much experience they have with Short Sales or Foreclosures? Pre-foreclosure situations are stressful enough. Working with a Realtor that has experience in these areas will help relieve some of your stress and get you through this rough time in your life.

Glossary of Real Estate Terms

Adjustable Rate Mortgage: A loan that allows the interest rate to be changed periodically.

Agency: A legal relationship in which an owner engages a broker-agent in the sale of property or a buyer engages a broker-agent in the purchase of property.

Annual Percentage Rate: The total finance charge (interest, loan fees, and points) expressed as a percentage of loan amount.

Amortization: The gradual repayment of a mortgage by periodic installments.

Appraisal: An estimate of the value of the property at the time the appraisal was done.

Assessed Value: The value placed on a piece of property by a tax assessor being the basis for property taxes.

Balloon Mortgage: A mortgage that has a substantial amount of the principal due at the maturity of the note.

Broker: A person licensed by a state real estate commission to act independently in conducting a real estate brokerage business.

See Page 87 For Your Free Service Offer

Closing: The final step in transferring ownership of a property from seller to buyer.

Closing Costs: Fees and expenses, not including the price of the home, payable by the seller and the buyer at the time of closing (e.g., brokerage commissions, property taxes, title insurance, inspections and appraisal fees).

Condominium: Ownership, which involves a separation of property into individual ownership elements and common ownership elements.

Contingency: A condition that must be satisfied before a contract is binding. Normally the buyer needs to sell another piece of property.

Conventional Loan: A fixed-rate, fixed-term loan that is made without government insurance.

Deed: A legal document conveying title to a property.

Earnest Money: A payment given to the seller by a potential buyer indicating the buyer's intent to complete the purchase of the property.

Equity: The owner's value of interest in a property.

Escrow: The placement of money or documents with a third party for safekeeping pending the

See Page 87 For Your Free Service Offer

fulfillment or performance of a specific act or condition.

FHA Mortgage: A mortgage loan insured by the Federal Housing Administration, permitting lenders to offer better terms.

Fixed-rate Mortgage: A loan that has only one stated interest rate.

Forbearance: The mortgage lender allows a reduction on the past due amount and spread the missed payments out over a period of time.

Foreclosure: The bank repossesses the property due to lack of payment.

HOA: Home Owners Association.

HUD: Housing and Urban Development; A US governmental agency established to implement certain federal housing and community development programs.

Lien: A legal claim against a property that must be paid when the property is sold.

Loan Modification: The bank agrees to reduce the current loans principal, interest or monthly payment.

Loan Origination Fee: The charge you must pay a lender for processing you mortgage.

See Page 87 For Your Free Service Offer

Market Value: The highest price a ready, willing and able buyer will pay and the lowest price a seller will accept.

Mortgage: A lien on real estate given by the buyer as security for money borrowed from a lender.

MLS: Multiple Listing Service

Points: A dollar amount, expressed as a percentage of the mortgage amount, which is paid to a lender as consideration for making a loan. Also called discount points.

P&I: Principal and Interest; a periodic payment that includes the interest charges for the period plus an amount applied to amortization of the principal balance.

PITI: The periodic payment that includes a principal and interest payment plus a contribution to the escrow account set up by the lender to pay insurance premiums and property taxes on the mortgage property.

REALTOR: Registered collective membership marks that identify real estate professionals who are members of the National Association of REALTORS and subscribe to a strict Code of Ethics.

See Page 87 For Your Free Service Offer

Short Sale: The lender allows an owner to sell the property for a reduced amount of the current balance due.

Title: A document that is evidence of ownership.

Title Insurance: Protection for lenders and homeowners against financial loss resulting from legal defects in the title.

VA Mortgage: A mortgage loan guaranteed by the Veterans Administration, an agency of the federal government that provides services for eligible veterans.

See Page 87 For Your Free Service Offer

About The Author

Hello! I'm Trisha Miller, the Author of "How To Sell Your Own Home". I would like to take a few minutes to give you a little history of my real estate background. I have been a licensed Realtor since 1999 working in many aspects within the real estate profession. Some of these aspects included real estate sales, office management, transaction to close coordination, and included three years with the National Credit Union Administration in the Division of Asset Recovery specializing in foreclosures and REO properties.

Though my real estate license is in Texas, while with the National Credit Union Administration, I worked on real estate transactions in multiple states. In 2013 alone, I closed over 200 real estate transactions and have the knowledge to provide you with valuable information to help you successfully sell your own home, saving you thousands of dollars.

Thank you for purchasing my book and this is my gift to you. At any point, should you decide you would like to speak with a Realtor, I will be happy to talk with you about your needs; research, interview and refer a Realtor to you that can help you with your specific situation. There is no fee to you for this service; it is simply a time saving gift to thank you for purchasing my book. You can contact me at trisha@RealtorBiz101.com

I hope this book is beneficial in helping you sell your own home.

Sincerely,
Trisha Miller, Author, Realtor

See Page 87 For Your Free Service Offer